C000096095

Yield

Claire Dyer holds a BA in English & History from the University of Birmingham, an MA in Victorian Literature & Culture from the University of Reading and an MA in Creative Writing from Royal Holloway, University of London. She lives in Reading, Berkshire. *Yield* is her third collection.

By the same author

Poetry
Eleven Rooms, Two Rivers Press (2013)
Interference Effects, Two Rivers Press (2016)

Fiction
The Moment, Quercus (2013)
Falling for Gatsby, Quercus (2014)
The Perfect Affair, Quercus (2014)
The Last Day, The Dome Press (2018)

Also by Two Rivers Poets

William Bedford, *The Dancers of Colbek* (2020)
Kate Behrens, *Penumbra* (2019)
Conor Carville, *English Martyrs* (2019)
John Froy, *Sandpaper & Seahorses* (2018)
Maria Teresa Horta, *Point of Honour* translated by Lesley Saunders (2019)
Ian House, *Just a Moment* (2020)
Rosie Jackson & Graham Burchell, *Two Girls and a Beehive* (2020)
Sue Leigh, *Chosen Hill* (2018)
James Peake, *Reaction Time of Glass* (2019)
Peter Robinson & David Inshaw, *Bonjour Mr Inshaw* (2020)
Peter Robinson, *The Constitutionals: A Fiction* (2019)
Lesley Saunders, *Nominy-Dominy* (2018)
Jack Thacker, *Handling* (2018)
Jean Watkins, *Precarious Lives* (2018)

Yield

Claire Dyer

TWO RIVERS PRESS

First published in the UK in 2021 by Two Rivers Press
7 Denmark Road, Reading RG1 5PA.
www.tworiverspress.com

© Claire Dyer 2021

The right of the poet to be identified as the author of this work
has been asserted by her in accordance with the Copyright, Designs
and Patents Act of 1988.

All rights reserved. No part of this publication may be reproduced,
stored in or introduced into a retrieval system, or transmitted,
in any form, or by any means (electronic, mechanical, photocopying,
recording or otherwise) without the prior written permission
of the publisher.

ISBN 978-1-909747-84-5

1 2 3 4 5 6 7 8 9

Two Rivers Press is represented in the UK by Inpress Ltd
and distributed by NBNi.

Cover design and lettering by Sally Castle based on illustrations by Peter Hay
Text design by Nadja Guggi and typeset in Janson and Parisine

Printed and bound in Great Britain by Severn, Gloucester

Acknowledgements

With thanks to the editors of the following publications/websites who have featured poems in this collection, or versions of them: *Bath Writers & Artists*; *Bedford Square 7,* Ward Wood Publishing; *Finished Creatures*, issue one, 2019; *Finished Creatures*, issue three, 2020; *Soft Touch*, Reading Stanza; *Stanley Spencer Poems: An Anthology*, eds Jane Draycott, Carolyn Leder, Peter Robinson, Two Rivers Press, 2017; *Structo 19*, 2019; *Tales from our Town*, ed. Miranda Lloyd, Reading Writers, 2016; *The High Window*, 2017; *The Interpreter's House*, 61, 2016; *the North*, 57, 2017; *The Rialto*, 90, 2018.

I would also like to thank the organisers and judges for the following competition commendations and prizes: Live Canon International Poetry Prize 2018, for 'Storage'; *Mslexia* Poetry Competition 2016, for 'Some Guidance on Leaving'; National Poetry Competition Longlist 2016 for 'on the train the girl'; *The Interpreter's House*, Open House Competition 2018, for 'Doing Cartwheels at The Ritz'; Ware Poets Open Poetry Competition 2016, for 'Chinese Bowl'; 2019 Poetry Book Society & *Mslexia* Women's Poetry Competition for 'Like This'.

My grateful thanks also to Structo (https://structomagazine.co.uk) for nominating 'Call and Response' for the 2020 Forward Prize for Best Single Poem.

Some of these poems have also featured in the show *Lolita Paints her Toenails*, performed by High Wire Act: Claire Dyer, Lesley Saunders & Susan Utting at both Reading Fringe Festival in July 2018, and Poetry in Aldeburgh in November 2019.

'Chinese Bowl' and 'The Night She Slept with the Fish' appeared as part of the 'WRITE Where We Are NOW' project initiated by Carol Ann Duffy & Manchester Writing School at Manchester Metropolitan University in April 2020 in answer to the Coronavirus pandemic.

The cover illustrations are from original Peter Hay prints I purchased at the party celebrating 25 years of Two Rivers Press. My collection had been accepted for publication and the discovery of the prints was serendipitous. Friends at Two Rivers Press have identified the front cover image as a linocut from around 1999 when Peter was working on Rimbaud's 'The Drunken Boat' but it was never used in a book. Sally Castle's cover design and lettering have captured the essence of the collection perfectly.

Contents

*For Lucy
and her godfather, John Kelly*

Yield I

v tr
To give forth by a natural process.

Think of fields, an afternoon plump with chaff,
the yellow harvester monstering. Yield.

Think of rabbits running silent the way rabbits run
fearful through the stalks.

Imagine the farmer; shirtsleeves rolled, skin hot,
giving up his crop, its burden is

immutable, everlasting, kin – *grain*
under his fingernails – reap, winnow –

In this town

there's a waterfall of cloud
and I'm sixteen, kissing a boy
who'll leave on a train heading west.

I'm working in this town,
buying typewriter ribbon
in Broad Street, its

Etch A Sketch of shopfronts,
its skyline's mismatch
of ages. In this town

swans' necks snow-curve
as they cruise
the gunmetal river,

windows blaze brickwork
and tall chimneys back at us.
In this town are buskers

and a buffet of languages.
Someone's planted flowers
in hanging baskets.

I am waiting for my children
to be born in this town.
I remember them as commas in my belly.

They visit occasionally
from distant places, bringing
new people in the car with them.

In this town what changes
casts long shadows. We say
the word *home* to one another here.

Alchemy

At the point of alchemy, you
were unreadable,

petal-flutter, dodgem, spring –
all the limbs of you coiled tight.

Skin taut, my pelvis ached
with sharp beauty

as you bore down.
Your birth was boy, was

an unravelling, all the length
of you held up for me to see,

our eyes meeting the way
eyes do, not knowing then that here,

at this other end of alchemy,
was how it was meant to be.

These are the concerns
of the cartographer:

to draw you belonging places,
chart your solemn moments of travel,

chronicle the ruins you leave behind,
honour the complexities of hills,

trace your land's boundaries,
pity the infinities of loss;

to cradle the punctures in the skies the stars shine through,
paint an ocean for the flounder,

for the flounder to shelter in –
in the nightfall dark of the sea bed's sand –

teach you to love and risk delight,
let you get lost in it.

Voice

We went to Great Brickhill
for the comet, like it was a gift

I could bring home in my pocket.
My dad took a thermos of soup

and I wore hand-knitted woollens,
my thickest socks – my breaths

small and inexplicable puffs. Later,
when I believed in constellations,

I saw Aquarius as lovers
dancing the Paso Doble

in a corner of the Milky Way.
Flying over the ocean,

I flipped the blind, moved
my face into the window,

saw my mother alongside,
her blue dress billowing.

Now what matters most
is you on stage aged eight –

a bright arrow of a child –
singing in your one voice

enough to fill the sky
before the cast join in,

the way at night we see
star after star after star.

The Label Maker

has small hands,
can stitch hummingbird-quick,

favours wearing bright colours:
lime, cerise, aquamarine.

He carries a pop-up house in a velveteen bag,
is bald, shameless, has obsidian eyes.

See him wait outside M&S for the man to sit,
bend his head; see the coins,

the wire-haired dog. See the Label Maker's
cotton of heron-wing grey,

his label says *Homeless.*
See him follow a woman to a hotel door,

watch as she checks in.
He leans against a wall, stitches

her *Faithless* with silver thread.
See him at the chemist's with fabric on his lap

as the boy who once was loved
swallows methadone, hands back the plastic cup.

The word now is *Hopeless.*
See him later in your kitchen.

See your child. On the table
is a form for something ordinary.

See him make ready when they falter
at the gender box.

See the sun glint on his needle and his small hands.
See your honeycomb heart shatter, fall.

Of Angels, Porcelain and Paint

Imagine a room, square windows
letting in the light. Imagine the light

is bright and yellow and falling
across rows of tables in slabs

the colour of butter. At the tables angels
are painting porcelain sunflower seeds –

the husks of sunflower seeds that is –
and, in the falling yellow light,

focus on a pigment each: pink, green,
russet, caramel, grey.

They take breaks at regular intervals,
stretch their necks and talk about the news –

somewhere a war is ending,
another about to start;

how can they survive all this?
And, on one particular, peculiar,

sun-drenched day Stanley comes,
and they give him their creations,

give him baskets brimming
with painted seeds for his collage

of two figures (daughter
and father) harvesting leeks.

He bends Kathleen to her task.
She can smell soap,

her father's gardener's skin
is surprisingly clean and,

if you listen carefully
you can hear a torrent of birdsong;

clouds are holding in the rain.
Imagine then you are walking

into the room with the square windows
and the light that's bright and yellow

and falling, and Stanley says,
You can stir your fingers through the seeds

if you like, make billions of shifting pictures,
all uniquely yours.

Delusion is an Unspeakable Thing

In this rare, trembling quiet,
through the veins in my wrist and
rise of a colossal moon, it is flowering,

stem fragile as glass, tasting
as lime tastes – sudden, sharp then gone.
With it is the silence of unallowable distances.

Outside the house, globes of white light
are dropping from the street lamps
into kerb water and what I want to say

is a reservoir. In the darkness beyond,
petals are folding like fingers fold.
I had not meant it to be like this.

Clinic I

That first time you were boy
and I had five things

to say, casting them
one by one on the way:

car, train, tube,
Starbucks, waiting room.

I wonder if you knew
the violence of my holding on,

feet on the bank, leaning
over water, you

a frantic salmon in my hands.
In Reception, a woman

my age in a scarlet dress
that didn't fit

arrived just after us.
If I'd been braver, wiser,

kinder, the sixth thing
I would have asked

was if she'd thought of wearing
a petticoat under it.

Fury

The quick-fingered boy stands knee-deep in the thick water.
The fish I'll catch will be furious, he says.
The fish will be.

He knows if the fish is furious then all will be well
but the world will end anyway so
he tells himself he believes in God – this is a monstrous, shining lie.

I say, *Cover me with all your brilliant hands*
and in the morning the fireflies will blow out the candles on their backs,
tuck their heads under their wings and sleep. Somewhere it will be raining.

Oh God! In the thick water the boy's fish is furiously dying.
If you love me enough, he says,
you will comb the furious seas in this savage darkness.

Fireflies

It's three in the morning and, seeing that I'm up, your father asks
if I can get his bathrobe from the hook on the bedroom door
and tuck it over him because he's cold. It's January.
The wind is something vicious, a fox is keening
in next door's garden and sleep is hard – there are such burdens;
we shoulder them and they spill their damage,
damage moving across the ground as mercury moves.

I get the robe and place it over him, climb into bed, find
under the covers the belt's still in my arms. I pull at it, know
it's only static but in the dark it pulses tiny silver flares, like fireflies
lighting up the room with a moment's blessing. He's sleeping now,
turned away, as the sparks fade to being almost-never-there;
both moment and the benediction gone. The fox is howling still.
I think of her eyes glinting amber under this fierce high moon.

Delivery

A catcher of foxes standing,
a fox hanging from his hand,
his fist around its tail,

its head slack, blood spotting
the snow. The window open
to this, me leaning out,

naked, sore from the birth
and giddy with it. Did
I mention the snow,

and the garden lit
by a round white moon?
The tableau –

white moon, white snow, blood,
black pearls of fox eyes,
fox-catcher eyes; fox fur

shades of tangerine, caramel,
peach. I could see the pink
shine of the fox catcher's tongue

when he spoke. *It's a dog fox,*
a tod fox, reynard. I'll leave him here,
he said, letting the fox

fall to a soft thud of snow.
Somewhere, the quiet flight of owls,
the oil-slick dark of water – frozen,

last year's leaves. And I ran,
ran with bare arms, my breasts
bare, the fox catcher gone,

the fox dead at my feet
turned vixen, her belly
plump with young.

A Difference of Opinion

I say what
night is this –

this night of
the slow flight

of owls, of
the light-lows

below trees
and hill-

hollows; this
night of

the slow calls
of owls – the

sounds of high-
lows that tell

how day follows
and rain falls.

You say what
night is this

that we rise
slow from to

take the flight,
the sounds of

owls from to
banish the

dark-lows of
nights like this.

Delft, Two Spanish Wine Bottles and Chinese Tea Set

After the funerals and house clearance
we brought it here.

He said, *It's about the looking,*
not the seeing. Study the flaws

in the porcelain, the fragile shadows
that move as you move, and the angle

of the shelf, the small details of colour,
brushstroke, intent; the light's shining

from the right, and you could,
if you wish, wrap your hand

around the handle of the pot,
it'd be surprisingly heavy to lift.

There were days when
I didn't stop. I carried babies,

plates, some kind of hopefulness;
had photographs glued to my heart

and lines from half-forgotten songs
on my tongue.

Trans

-port is this, a way of travel or the travel to rapture;
-lation is this, our talk so they understand it:

the handbook tells us our journey will be fast and long,
the stars far, flung; we will scatter them

as we pass, not stop to hear them scream.
On landing we will learn gravity, yearn for home,

look for pairings: the rare birds – white,
mysterious, majestic, which mate for life;

look for strange: the rare boys and girls
who shape-shift and move on.

The handbook has no drawings of this.

-ition is this, the shape-shift and move on:

and there are those they call mother who sometimes stand
triumphant, waving banners from high places;

sometimes hide in corners, hearts splintering
the carpet. We are told not to worry,

we are the lucky ones: our talk needs no deciphering –
we have the gift of knowing without saying,

of saying without knowing; we are already both
boy and girl and we are neither; our love is unconditional.

The handbook has many drawings of this.

A Short History of Film

I

In Hollywood we sat on directors' chairs smoking fat cigars,
were seen at premieres wearing fox fur,
white dresses with wide skirts,
diamanté clips in our peroxide hair.

II

In the days of usherettes we wept
as Trevor Howard's train pulled out,
as Bogart said, *Here's looking at you, kid*;
as *ET* went home.

III

In our phones are videos of cats sleeping in the sun.
We post them and our hopes on Facebook,
get five *Likes* for our hopes,
seventy-two for the cats.

IV

In the days before film we knew more,
drew stick figures that leant in,
touched faces, leant out:
the story of love as a flicker book,

whichever way it went.

Pantomime

The usherette's torch is doing its lighthouse thing,
the players are whispering in the stalls over fizzy drinks
and bags of sweets about the truth in magic carpets,

and the Genie – an androgynous ventriloquist –
is holding up his magic lamp as though it is a hand grenade,
and Widow Twankey – splendid breasts strapped

like occasional tables to his chest – is scolding his best son
– a girl in boots and tights – for loving me, and the orchestra
drums are sounding and the audience is roaring, *Oh no, he doesn't.*

Bearded

From the stalls I watched
the spotlight as you launched your lines,

followed the tiny arcs of spit that bloomed
then fell away like fireworks do.

Your body was something familiar;
your walk and voice I recognised

from every before, and here on stage
you were bearded, suited, marvellous;

a professor from Montreal
weary of the world's intrigues,

love's colours and its bedazzlements.
And, as you acted the brilliant shattering

of your heart, I wept – not for love
or the lack of it – but because

I could not tell if, beneath your skin,
you were slowly suffocating.

Some Guidance on Leaving

Come, sadness tells me, put on the yellow dress
and pack a bag with useful things:
a pair of angel's wings, a cup of rain
last night's storm flung against the house,
the scent of sun, all you once believed.
Take your keys to the river's edge.
Watch the grasses and the river birds,
feel the hands of the man you love span
the slope of your back the way they used to do.
Hold the keys in your fist until the metal burns –
it should be evening, March maybe and after the clocks,
the sky surprised that it's light like this –
cast it all into the water,
count your steps as you walk away.

As Shepherd

I'll keep sheep,
wear Aran sweaters,
drink Glenfiddich out of a tin cup.

My desk will watch the sea,
and two gulls banking
at forty-five degrees against a sky

the colour of raw pastry.
I'll grow cabbages
and barter them for eggs

to make omelettes from;
listen to the shipping news
on screech-owl nights when

the moon is cast like fishing floats
in all the standing water in my yard.
I'll have no telephone,

will learn weather and the language
of dog; not mind the lack of dainty,
mown lawns, pedicures, but

on the end-papers of a novel
I've already read I'll write
the lines from which all the world's

poems will spawn; will take the pages,
burn them, the book and this
in a brazier in an April field

before the sun has gone and
before the stars,
my sheep looking on.

I wrote your names

with a knife on my heart and voiced them
in black ink and blue ink I typed texted

and dreamt the names you were meant to pass on
that you've passed on now you have names

I can't say because try as they might they're not in my chest like
the rest that are still holding fast to the bones

in my back and my neck and my mouth is full
of dry grasses rivers and trees

The Trough

See it in a field somewhere in a dark country.
Its metal is pitted, rust blooming through

in places into latticework or lace,
or the foam at the edges of small waves.

In it is weather and language, chaos, hope;
all the first thoughts and the last.

In it is rainwater and the bodies of dead creatures.
I've known those who've used it for target practice,

lined up bottles on its rim, taken pot shots;
green glass, red wine exploding like tracer fire.

At night, when no-one's looking,
cattle rub their fragrant bodies against it.

Around it the mud is rutted with dung,
a few crushed daisies.

I'll look in it tomorrow,
if the love allows.

Doing Cartwheels at The Ritz

Walk in like you own the place, I said and,
leaving the low hum of Piccadilly behind us

we did, and sat in chairs like thrones,
ordered wine which came in glasses

as wide as our cupped hands.
As we drank we laughed – the carousel

of baby grand and waiting staff nodding
small and tight to one another

as they passed by. In time, two perfect people
on the catwalk of the main salon:

stylish, moneyed, wearing tiaras of happiness.
Husband. Wife. In front of them, a child –

a cream lace dress – doing cartwheels
down the centre aisle as though this was a parade

and they the spectacle the crowds
had been waiting for. We smiled,

our years together bursting through
the mirrored walls in licks of magenta flame.

Cinematic and extravagant, we saw your birth,
first words and steps, the skim of stones

on a turquoise sea, your awkward
boyhood years. *Come*, I said, *let's do the same*

and, putting down our drinks we did:
through the onlookers,

through the music, the towers of flowers,
all the chandelier light of that particular,

wondrous night, you and I did cartwheels at the Ritz,
setting free the inner girl in both of us.

Clinic II

That second visit you were girl and
I had less to say.

Like it was usual, your dad and I
drank tea nearby,

returned to hear you plan
next time for a person

known by your new name,
your new voice ringing with it,

bouncing it off the walls, ruffling
the leaflets on the notice boards.

After you another girl –
going the other way – asking

for her next appointment
to be later in the day.

She had a distance to travel,
no family, money, love.

If I'd been braver, wiser,
kinder, I'd have given her

enough for a hotel, given him
a hot meal, hope, a hug.

What's True

You'd say she is magnificent for
she has shoulders. You'd be wrong though, for

if you take scalpel, draw curve on her chest, blood will pour,
flood the floor – the lonely blue floor,

and she is afraid of the revealing,
of the skin being pared and of the skin falling

into an initial like skin from an apple saying
what's true – embryoed and curling –

the bones in its spine small white discs of.

The Night She Slept with the Fish

Not that he, a fairground prize
from years ago, was in her bed,
his fins against her skin,

his fish lips fish-kissing her neck,
but rather in his tank on the other side
of the room and her a long way from home,

him shimmying from back to front,
from end to end through the dark hours
and the light hours, watching her grieve

with his fish eyes, his fish mouth
opening in an O and closing in a smile
like he was silent-singing

an Italian aria, the quiet
only broken by the soft wheeze
of the water pump and him rootling

now and then through the gravel,
searching for the kind of happiness
she'd once believed was hers,

each fruitless fish-dive
a confirmation that yearning
is the occupation of fools.

Coming Out I

You said the hardest part was telling us.
Standing – letter in hand – in an apocalypse of rain,
the moment thin as a blade, you tipping
the knife so raindrops rivered onto it,

clouds moving to make a picture of clouds,
and posting us your heart.
And now I'm on the doorstep of my parents' house.
I'm five, twelve, twenty-one,

can smell my mother's chutney –
the vinegar hit at the back of my throat –
Swarfega slicing through the grease
on my father's hands, how it lingers

on the skin. There are footsteps,
so many sundered dreams, war stories,
schooldays, old mornings, the zest
of fresh mown grass, the silence of closed doors.

I fear the bomb I hold in my mouth, can
already see the debris of torn limbs,
the fallout from a thorny kind of love,
hear them say they don't understand.

Lent

I will not window you,
not for the nights and days
it's going to take, the mornings

light pigeons the curtains
and words willow the back
of the postman's throat.

Just think how it'll start,
rain pancaking the pavements,
rooks' wings inside out,

leaf buds crazy, horse-
havoc in the fields. I will
eyelash during it, heart

with friends in coffee shops,
daffodil my face to the wind,
doors flung wide in the middle

of my chest. It will persist
and I will not, not window,
willow or word you, apparently.

Saturday

was laundry,
feeding the cats,
two calls to my sister,
writing this here,
the day's planes above the clouds –

was the Post Office queue,
(your text said,
Hey Mum, landing at seven)
a basket of groceries,
paying for the dry cleaning,
the *Johnsons'* boy's smile a surprise,
like a brief rip in the sky –

was the marshal at St Peter's
directing cars in his safety coat,
The Butterfly Preservation Society
on a chalkboard by his side –

was a house waiting
where once had been the sound
of something other than me
humming in the kitchen,
the purr of the central heating,
the twenty leaves on the Judas Tree
in its pot in the yard –

was driving to Heathrow to get you,
rain thick on the wiper blades,
and fireworks over Slough
for the festival of Eid.

Not a tragedy

is not how I see it, not
with this heart, these eyes

still seeing snatches
of sun and sandcastle cities

and Friday tea and algebra
and teaching you to read;

still the refrain of your key
in the door, some music,

and shirts drying on the line,
and the laughter we couldn't

breathe through because
it was blinding; still your wrists

and the running, your quiet
learning, how I didn't know;

how it has the weight of one
now there's nowhere

for the rest of it; the all
of seeing it still like this.

Storage

I see them soft-boned, new-skinned,
they are stars in jars
on laboratory shelves patterned

by a lattice of sun from an April day, or
a September one. I choose them all;
carry them in a universe of arms,

drawing in the talcum smell of them,
sweep of lashes, lip pucker,
and all the tiny of them. I follow

them to school, watch them line up
for prayers, the preciousness of knees,
elbows, chatter, light

folding itself blue into their eyes. I watch
them grow to girlhood, boyhood, woman,
man; they are not you, are you and

I remember the heave and push,
you birthing, my breasts spilling empty
for the full of you, and the fear is mighty

you will leave this final deed undone,
never know the pull of this exquisite love,
this love. This.

body clock I

always at 4.10   a goblin sits cross-legged on her chest   *why*   she asks   *why the skinny fingers why the size and weight of you   why come here again*   he smiles picks a piece of lint from underneath a nail   *I'm here to detonate your ribs*   he says   *make your mouth explode   I am the dreams you dare not dream*   she cannot blink   *ha*   he says   *ha ha   and it will not end   you will not win*   she listens for the seconds danger heartbeats to subside   the goblin lays his head the Velcro skin of his face across her breasts   there is something almost sexual in the silent grace of this   she'd thought she'd learnt to recognise the way loss walks across the fields the taste of grief like lemons on her tongue   it is winter in the eucalyptus but a bird's out there his songs flaring in the dark   she says the word *vortex* to herself a thousand times as the bird sing-sings the goblin sleeps the night is fat with tick tock tick and she waits

body clock II

and she waits her eyes open to the dark   her cat is wailing in the road dreams talking in her mouth   her husband is asleep again and she thinks of daybreak how there's no actual rupture no sound of tearing or a sundering apart but rather an unfolding of the sky like someone's lighting a million energy-saving bulbs and they're slowly brightening   the taste of her dreams is fading but still she is afraid of what she cannot see so leaves the goblin snoring and in what lamp glow there is from the street walks along the landing to the stairs the cat is halfway down them or halfway up and is looking at her with his yellow eyes   she will make tea in her favourite mug switch on the TV and watch it without the volume up and there will be seconds danger heartbeats as outside dawn becomes irrevocable and the cat will no doubt go outside again

body clock III

Tick tock body clock.
Put it in a box

to make it stop.
Tell the clock gob-

lin to hop
it. Your heart, lob it –

far, toss
it from the shore –

ignore the furor-
e when you tell the tick tock

gob-lin to swap
love for what's not;

instead, trot off
and shed the lot:

the tick-tock gob-
lin swap hop-

ping sea shore furore.
Tick tock body clock.

Fuck the gob-
lin. Rock it.

Parcel Post

It arrived one morning
wrapped in brown paper
and tied with string

like a package from the past.
I left it in the kitchen
for an hour or so

as I set about my chores,
mantra-muttering the I-can-
cope-without-it talk.

Around noon I weakened,
carried it upstairs and laid it
on my bed. Its opening was thunder

in the silence of the house, and
holding it to the light, it shone.
Pearlescent, magnificent, it caught

the sun in its folds, throwing
that light the colour of butter
on the floor. If I'd had a choice,

I would have picked peacock-blue,
but the only option was
flesh-gold, like the stockings

Nan used to wear. The seconds ticked –
the way that seconds do –
as I stripped bare to reveal

my most marvellous scars,
the sad surfaces that need repair.
I slipped it on. It was a perfect fit.

The label said, *Thick Skin –*
tailor-made, but somehow
still it lets the arrows in.

Wardrobe

If we were in a movie
there'd be woodland creatures

at my feet, a sun
glitterballing a lake nearby.

I'd have a tiny waist, cascade of hair,
my neck would arc like a swan's. Yes,

if we were in a movie
there'd be squirrels on the window sill,

rabbits bouncing gleeful
on the bed, bluebirds fluttering

the clothes you don't now need
away in their beaks.

The suits would go,
the shirts, underpants, socks,

homeless folk would be clothed,
wrongs made right,

charity shop windows bejewelled. Yes,
if we were in a movie

I'd be singing, not weeping
the way I'm weeping as

I pack away the tiny jacket – its galaxy
of swimming badges

sewn on once upon a time
when you were still a boy.

Chinese Bowl

Moments before, I hold it against the day's pearl light.
There are tulips in a vase on the kitchen table.
So much of the house is silence.
The bowl's the size of my cupped hands,
has the translucency of small water
stitched at the edge of the incoming tide.
Its blue is indescribable. There are tiny veins in its glaze.
And, when I let it fall it lands with the sound
of applause. I step on the pieces
with bare feet thinking there must be
some kind of pain in the joy of this.
Later I'll gather the fragments;
wash blood from each one with care,
try to decide where the beauty is.

Yield II

v intr
To give up, as in defeat; surrender or submit.

Plump light today, early and
falling in bandwidths wider
than heartbeats. I am taking

photographs of small corners
and wood polish; pictures
of glint and shadow, the still lives of daffodils,

chairs, the mirror the garden's fallen into. Yield.
I am yielding, standing in the hallway
where the clock is talking now,

the stairs silently travelling, the carpet
holding echoes the size of stars.
In each room there's a moment like leaf-fall.

Flock

First to come was a linnet.
She asked if she could stay
and each day we'd sing a little,
then she'd fly out the open door,
fly in the turquoise air.
Next came a thrush, two starlings, a wren.
Soon I had a flock.
I read sonnets to them as they preened,
burnished their beaks
with cotton buds, tucked diamonds
under their wings and,
when we were enough,
we stitched us a blanket of birds,
warmed you with our hundred tiny hearts.

on the train the girl

in the blue satin dress is beauty tonight
he asks *is this seat taken*   she answers *feel free*

he's in black tie   tells her
dinner at The Savoy

she replies *out with friends*
his eyes are golden

teeth very white   she looks away
and her face is in the window

outside is completely dark
he taps *I'm married* on her arm

and when he speaks his beard ripples
when he moves his body is mutable

lithe   a savannah wind stirs the star grass
and the lemon grass at their feet

she nods *I ran away to the circus now fly the trapeze*
study lion taming one evening a week

the woman opposite is knitting
with alpaca wool   her needles click-click

he pushes back his jacket sleeve
licks his dark lion lips as the tannoy

says they're at Maidenhead
the skin on his wrist is pelt

she places a fingertip on the thick soft fur
some people stare

on the train the girl has wine for blood
and music in her hair   says

I've trained a hawk
and dived for pearls

Letting Go of the Mammoth

I take him from my bag,
set him down on the kitchen floor.

He blinks his mammoth eyes,
lashes long enough to sweep up dust,

ears surprising, small,
twitching the way gazelles' ears do.

He's spent a while down deep
with the elastic bands and ticket stubs,

has been somewhat weighty but
good as gold, and now's his time,

so I watch him take his first slow steps,
all wobble, stumble, weave.

He lifts his trunk to the scent of bacon,
milk, frail human dreams.

I want to give him ocean-air,
tundra, temperatures

cold enough for snow,
long to see him run.

When a loss is not a loss

it's as heavy as, and as long as, has
a pond-skater's balance, its feet
poised on the surface of, the sudden stop
and start, the hurry to and from; is
the waxy hearts of water lilies; is
a bell – as in church bell
after the pull-down-and-release –
you, can you hear it echoing?;
is a muntjac dying slowly roadside wrapped
in a stranger's coat – broken headlights
on the tarmac – the stranger waiting
for the impossible, for the deer to stand,
scent the air for danger, disappear into the trees
steady on its brilliant hooves.

Call and Response

Then there was the time
when the grief was tremendous

and she stopped in a Devon lane,
left the car and stood instead

at a gate looking out onto the glittering
fields – the late summer fields –

at the inexplicable ruins
of farms – ancient walls beginning

and ending without reason –
some distant sheep,

and listened to nothing more than
the pulse in her ears,

the rolling wind, a kestrel's call,
its mate's answering cry.

Easter Break

Then there was the week you came back
to the rhythm the house taps out in bricks
and windows when it knows you're here.

In your bag: mascara, heels, the bear
you've slept with since you were five,
your padded bra, all the words of yours

we've spoken leaving your mouth an octave
higher than before, me, seeing you as you are,
moving so much less than boy, so much more.

Then you, a sudden beard again, in pyjamas I,
mother-of-a-son, have washed, washed, pegged
times without number on the line. Then you,

that last bright morning,
smooth-skinned and smiling,
the girl you are walking out the door.

Shopping

Let us go then, you and I, to Primark, Zara, Reiss.
The sky'll be brilliant and,

around us, shoppers will burst into song,
dance on the up escalators and the down

as we load our arms with gorgeousness,
lacework brushing our shins.

The colours will dazzle us.
On the concourse outside Dune

trombonists will lift their instruments
heavenward, shatter the ceiling.

Violinists in the doorway of New Look
will draw their bows like waves

ceaselessly breathing. A ballerina
next to Top Shop will pirouette,

we'll watch her head spin, arms
held gracious as the petals on a rose,

and I will ask if you've ever thought of Wallis
and you'll say *Give over, Mum,*

that's for old women, not for me.
Oh, what a beautiful morning it will be.

On Arrival

When I get there the country will be run by dragons, and seagulls
   will have learnt to waltz.
When I get there butterflies will live forever.
When I get there all trains will run on time.
When I get there silver spoons will abound.
When I get there no one will litter, graffiti will only be on display
   in museums, it'll be Banksy's face on ten pound notes.
When I get there chocolate won't make me fat.
When I get there raindrops will be lilac, grass able to talk.
When I get there horses will live in houses
   and take afternoon tea at five.
When I get there all it'll take is an outstretched hand, palm up,
   and there'll be peace in the world.
When I get there the woman at number 54 will have taken in
   her washing, put the potatoes onto boil.
When I get there someone will have captured birdsong in a jar.
When I get there I will have chosen the words to say what needs
   to be said.

Spill

I Study for

Mackerel are shoaling the blue waters.
There's a docker dividing a clamour of human hearts

into wire baskets on the quay.
I watch the growth knots on the clematis in my garden loosen.

In the tiny are vast, inexplicable things.
The first thoughts will be of birdsong captured in a jar.

With practice I'll write the splitting of glass,
the spill of the song.

II Spill

She lifts the jar with her pale hands,
her pale fingers,
her fingernails mother-of-pearl pale.

She twists the jar in an act of refraction
to the point where light splits,
waits –

waits for the heat to build,
the first cracks to appear.
The sun is at its absolute.

And then they come: hesitant, sinewy,
like moments before deer run,
and soon the sound is deafening;

the foretaste of apocalypse.
So the glass shatters, blasts tiny
red stitches into the skin

on her arms, her face,
yet still the glass glints,
yet still the light splits.

And, at last, the song spills
in a song waterfall.
The birds know exactly what they do.

Coming Out II

This grass is blistering in the heat,
is brittle underfoot as I answer the door
to my father ready to say

what's been in my mouth so long
it's hard to know when it began.
I've rehearsed, the words moving

across my tongue like marbles
in a drum. Act it, I tell myself.
Think stage lights, greasepaint,

Mavis selling ice creams
at the break. I keep the saying of it short:
the how, when, why, pledge

nothing will really change. And
then the pause, a silence vast enough
to swallow all of time,

each mountain, tree,
fern, salmon
leaping up the fall.

Prayer

Incremental change – brilliant,
brave and burgeoning:

skin, voice, gait,
hips, waist, breasts,

your cobalt eyes
seeming a shade darker than before.

You've prayed for this, waited
a thousand days for it to start.

I join you at the altar now –
supplicant, mother, friend.

Clinic III

You entered like a gazelle –
graceful, eyes wide and oh, so lovely.

The stairwell air was homely.
We're getting used to this, your father said.

I tried not to stare, feel
the sharp points of others' needs

lodged in the corners of the room.
When you were called, we went to Pret

and I watched a woman from the clinic
buy a Swedish Meatball Wrap,

a dustcart inch along Fulham Palace Road –
man in high-vis jacket picking up

the trash – knots of kids
walking home from school,

a couple at the bus stop kiss and,
if I'd been braver, wiser, kinder, I

Not Dancing

When I get to
the end of this I

will tell you
what I missed

will wait
in a town near

beauty parlours
post boxes

coffee shops
watch people

in the clothes
they'll wear

that morning
the yellow shirt

the socks skirt dress
marvel how

boys choose some-
times to be girls

girls boys
be astounded

by the stories
the countless

shining joys and
ticking in my head

will be all the hours
I spent not dancing

Correspondence

Say I write *Do you remember* and list how once I held
the hands of children who, a time ago, were mine;
how I listened to the long exhale of oceans
when the sun was spilling yellow
across the sand, across the covert feathers of sea birds
in flight; how I ate and, in the pause between courses,
spoke what was best left unsaid;
how the weather was when he and I were not yet lovers,
how afterwards we watched the moon allow the fields
outside the window to become themselves.
Say I leave the letter too late for the years to find,
leave it at rest against a vase of blue geraniums,
a gift unread in the glittering light of a hallway,
the shadows of a staircase falling across a wide, bright floor.

Say

it's the only way to place the burning of the loss of those who never grow to know that endings, earth and cypress trees are any otherwise than this. Say it's for those who remain outside the frame, reaching for the vanished hand, for the words hope-beauty-love again, again. Say it's spark and jet and flame, the way light blazes the darkling water, how water closes over you when you're drowning, opens when you're coming up for air.

Separation

She hurls words at it in peat, steel, Pharaoh's gold; is carried on the spine of a thought as impossible as mercury, can remember his bones move under the flat of her hand.

For now she is liminal, her language is churn, is foam and horizontal; she has the power of naming stuck in the back of her throat, will trace the mast of a bruise taller than the vocabulary of her heart at the place where the sky hurts most, step into the waves, swim the terrible distance.

Clinic IV

This time on your own,
me, a pearl in your pocket,
promise for us both.

Abracadabra

It's the first thing they ask;
the how, when, what and where of it

firecrackers from their mouths,
my heart shudders, and

flares fly from my eyes.
I take a blade, saw them in half,

conjure them into toads,
make them disappear.

*

I know this alchemy is yours,
but in my dreams it's sorcery –

a magician pulling a white dove,
startled, from a hat.

*

See this wizard-surgeon's
cape swirl, how

his wand glints
in the hard, electric light.

My teeth ache at this no going back.
I will feel each incision, stitch,

be there when you wake.

Memoir

And then that Christmas:
my father, his new granddaughter,

talking memoir, science, cures –
how once he'd saved my brand-new life;

me cooking, my mother there,
my husband, son, and

daughter-in-law-to-be listening
to you speak in the quiet

of this brave new world.

Sand

I see you at your brother's wedding,
your heads together like you as infants

sitting side by side sifting sand
at the garden's end on elastic afternoons

under the antique apple tree,
the cat looking on.

You'd both be lost in the magic,
the science of heap and scrape,

of plastic truck, rampart, soldier, art.
Seen from the kitchen, you

were beacons, summer gold threading
your gold hair, your talk silent,

folded into curve of shoulder,
arm, the soft arches

of your naked feet.
It could never last –

one of you would err,
there'd be tears, and I'd soothe

or scold, marshal either, both of you,
move the moment on

to here, you together, this
horizontal light, this bay,

below us a carpet of stars, grains
of sand glinting *quartz, rose, and amethyst.*

Abroad

the waiters mistake us for sisters.
No, we say, laughing.

We know they know we're not,
but we're more than

who we seem. We're
every boy moment, every girl,

the way sunlight falls like nectar
on the stairs. We're crockery-chime,

every mile, leaf, bird-flight, song.
Under our feet the street is evening-warm,

the call to prayer rises as smoke
rises and drowns the town.

Your name is Lucy,
it tastes of spice and wine –

kimyon, sumac, Lal –
fills my mouth with sparks.

On the day your father and I
do almost everything

we wake snug in the lungs of an ocean,
he touches me and afterwards

we breakfast – ravenously.
Later, we visit galleries,

take pictures of light switches
next to the paintings because they,

the switches – not the paintings –
seem like art. We buy chips and

sit on a bench *in memory of.*
On the beach seagulls quarrel,

and still the sea is breathing.
Going for ice cream, we meet

families – their children sudden
reminders – and he and I

share a cone – he says he remembers
his mother's mixing bowl,

the taste of Sunday afternoons –
a bit like, but not like,

this Sunday afternoon.
As the sun sets we walk the wetlands –

blue boats, blue clouds –
and even later, as the moon

spills across the sea towards us –
but before the fishermen –

we find a daughter on the shoreline
resting in a nest of stones.

I raise her to my breast where she suckles,
then sleeps. In the distance is the glow

of the wind farm's tiny yellow eyes and,
near to midnight, we unwrap her

from her shawl which, in this light,
is made from fabric that looks unearthly,

and see her legs are not legs but a fish's tail,
the scales purpling and silvering.

She wakes and cries, anxious to be gone,
so we take her to the waves,

and the last thing we see is her –
a brightness in the brightness

of the spilling moon – balancing
all our glad hearts in hers.

Storm Warning

The elements bickering and me –
between slices of wakefulness –

dreaming of being brittle-boned;
my fear, me saying

I don't know you, I had two sons,
this girl is a confusion.

And, daughter, if I do,
line the pockets of my best winter coat

with stones and take me
to the water's edge,

leave me slowly walking
into the surf.

Yield III

v tr
To supply or produce something positive.

You are being unborn.
The midwife, careful with the brand-new of your limbs,
is folding you up.

I glance just once as she unsevers the cord;
am numb from gas and air and joy,
do not feel you slip back in.

My cervix closes behind you with a hush,
I am walking backwards to the car and
the rain is falling up.

Bit by bit, you shrink, unform,
until your arms and legs are buds,
your heart the size of an apple pip,

and it's when we start all this,
one spring night in all the many,
one moment in the dark, and

I'm looking up to count the fearless stars,
choosing you once more,
a thousand times again. Yield.

Afterword: Like This

Each morning the stirring branches
and the shepherd calling his ribbon

of sheep to heel in the olive grove
beneath our window.

The bay scattered with tin-foil confetti,
the fishing boats bringing back the catch,

and in town they will be washing down
the restaurant floors, loading sweet peppers,

strawberries, aubergines into vans.
As the muezzin rings the air, a ballet

of bee-eaters rises above the trees.
You, my love, are with us here and,

turning, I see your father sleeping.
I did not expect it could still be like this.

Notes

'Yield I' – lines in italics have been taken from 'Harvesting', *Interference Effects*, Claire Dyer, Two Rivers Press, 2016.

'In this town' was commissioned by the Museum of Reading as part of the 2016 'Sense of Place' exhibition, in response to John Piper's tapestry, 'Townscape'.

'The Label Maker' first appeared in *Interference Effects*, Claire Dyer, Two Rivers Press, 2016.

'Of Angels, Porcelain and Paint' is after 'Gardening, 1945', The Stanley Spencer Gallery, and Ai Weiwei, 'Sunflower Seeds, 2010', Tate Modern, and was published in *Stanley Spencer Poems: An Anthology*, eds Jane Draycott, Carolyn Leder, Peter Robinson, Two Rivers Press, 2017.

'Delft, Two Spanish Wine Bottles and Chinese Tea Set' is by Christopher Harrison, 1971.

In 'Bearded', the play referred to is 'Strawberries in January' by Évelyne de la Chenelière.

'Shopping', the first line comprises words from 'The Love Song of J. Alfred Prufrock,' by T.S. Eliot.

'Correspondence' is after 'The Bight' by Elizabeth Bishop, *A Cold Spring*, 1955.

'Say' is after 'Isle of the Dead' by Arnold Böcklin.

'Separation' is after 'Coastline of Catterline' by Joan Eardley.

'Abroad': *kimyon, sumac, Lal* are Turkish for cumin, a tangy lemon spice, and a make of wine.

The last lines of 'Delusion is an Unspeakable Thing', 'Not a tragedy' and 'Like This' were inspired by 'Eden Rock' by Charles Causley, *Collected Poems*, 2000.

Two Rivers Press has been publishing in and about Reading since 1994. Founded by the artist Peter Hay (1951–2003), the press continues to delight readers, local and further afield, with its varied list of individually designed, thought-provoking books.